# THUD! THUD!



Written by Diana Aleksandrova

Illustrated by Svilen Dimitrov

ISBN: 978-1-953118-10-3
Library of Congress Control Number: 2020920241

Illustrations by Svilen Dimitrov

First Printing Edition 2020

Check out more of Diana's work on her website:
www.dedonibooks.com

The magic of books Dedoni LLC

To my family and to all of you, who love stories as much as I do! - D. A.

To Alisa and Alexander, who inspire me every single day! - S. D.

The forest buzzed with the chatter of cheerful creatures. The animals lived there happily in peace and harmony. They spent their days playing games and collecting food..

Until one day...

A loud sound shook the ground.
"A monster has moved in," a bunny whispered.
"A terrible, terrible monster!" a squirrel chattered.
The news spread quickly.

The animals began living in fear of the terrifying monster.
Life in the forest was forever changed.

The squirrels,
who were storing food for the winter,
stopped their work when they heard the sound.
They looked down at two pointy horns,
squeaked, and scrambled to hide up in the branches of the tree.

A few acorns landed on the ground. The monster jumped and looked around wide-eyed.

PLOP!

The deer was grazing on grass,
when she heard the sound.

The frightened deer
dashed through the forest,
breaking branches on her way.
The monster shuddered and ran in the opposite direction.

The bunnies were playing who-can-hop-the-highest,
when they suddenly perked up
their long ears at the sound.

The ground shook.

The terrified bunnies dove into their burrow.

The monster gasped and tried to follow the bunnies into the safety of their tiny home.

"Whooo, whooo," called the owl, spotting the monster creeping along in the dark. The monster whimpered and jumped behind a tree to hide.

WHOOo
WHOOO

"We have to move to a place with no terrible monsters!"

the animals agreed.

"I have to move to a place without scary creatures!" the monster thought.

The monster took a sip of water from the river.
Suddenly, he was face to face with a furry head
and a pair of pointy horns.
Two big eyes looked back at him.
He had never seen such a scary monster!

"MONSTER! MONSTER!" he shrieked, racing through the forest.
THUD! THUD! went his heavy steps.
The forest echoed with the cry of "MONSTER! MONSTER!"
and the booming sound of THUD! THUD!

Frightened, the squirrels chattered and darted up a tree where they crashed right into the sleeping owl. They all plummeted together, landing on the opening of the bunnies' home right before the poor bunnies could get in. The deer tripped on them and tumbled down. Soon enough, All the animals in the forest were piled together.

On top of them was the monster shedding huge monster tears,
heaving huge monster sobs, and covering his eyes
with his huge monster hands.

One by one, the animals pulled themselves up and
took cover behind the nearby trees.

The loud sobs made
them peek out from their hiding places.

They stared at the weeping monster.

First, the bunny hopped over to the sobbing monster and cautiously patted him on the back.
"There, there, now. It's okay."
The monster opened one eye.
His crying subsided.
Seeing the bunny was unharmed, the others approached the scared monster too.
"Don't be afraid."
"We won't hurt you!"
"We can be friends!"

The monster sniffed a last giant sniff and wiped his last, large tear. He looked around at all the animals and smiled shyly.

THUD! THUD! The ground shook. But instead of running and hiding, the animals would come out to greet their new monster friend.

THUD THUD, the big, skittish monster, was a little less frightened by every little sound or shadow, because now he knew that there were no scary creatures - only friends, in his new home.

Once again, the forest buzzed with the happy chatter of cheerful creatures.

Made in the USA
Middletown, DE
17 October 2023

40975874R00018